The Essential Bu

RANGE R(

THIRD
GENERATION

L322 2002 to 2012

Your marque expert:
James Taylor

VELOCE PUBLISHING
THE PUBLISHER OF FINE AUTOMOTIVE BOOKS

www.veloce.co.uk

First published in September 2019 by Veloce Publishing Limited, Veloce House, Parkway Farm Business Park, Middle Farm Way, Poundbury, Dorchester DT1 3AR, England. Tel +44 (0)1305 260068 / Fax 01305 250479 / e-mail info@veloce.co.uk / web www.veloce.co.uk • www.velocebooks.com.
ISBN: 978-1-787115-01-9; UPC: 6-36847-01501-5

British Library Cataloguing in Publication Data – A catalogue record for this book is available from the British Library.
Typesetting, design and page make-up all by Veloce Publishing Ltd on Apple Mac. Printed in India by Replika Press.

Introduction
– the purpose of this book

The aim of this book is to help you buy a third generation or L322 Range Rover that suits your needs and budget. It doesn't have to be in like-new condition, but it does have to be the best you can find within your budget, so that you get the best possible value for money. If you want to treat it as a pampered 'classic,' then that's great news. On the other hand, if you just want to enjoy owning and running it as an everyday vehicle, than that's fine. There's another dimension to ownership, too. These Range Rovers have quite astonishing off-road ability, and, in my view, it would be a shame to own one and never find out just how capable it is.

The third generation Range Rover was developed in the late 1990s, at a time when Land Rover was owned by BMW. That's why the first models had BMW engines; in fact, a great deal of the engineering development was done in Germany, although by Land Rover's own engineers. Under BMW it was known by the project code of L30, but when BMW sold Land Rover to Ford in 2000 (with the new Range Rover not yet released), the company's new owners gave it their own project code. So it became L322.

The Range Rover was already firmly established at the top of the luxury 4x4 market by the time work started on this one. It had a tough act to follow, and, with BMW's help, Land Rover designed it with the largest monocoque (one-piece body structure) that had ever been made up to that point. This improved refinement, and also represented a leap forward in technology, which was an important sales point for many Range Rover buyers. Cutting-edge technology would remain an important element in the Range Rover's appeal as it was developed further during a production run that lasted until 2012.

It's important to recognise that this cutting-edge technology was expensive,

The first production Range Rover ...

and, unless maintained to the manufacturer's recommendations, could become unreliable. The L322 does not take kindly to being run by owners who skimp on maintenance, and will reward them appropriately. But when it is maintained as intended, it is quite a remarkable piece of machinery, and one to enjoy and treasure. Regardless of who you are or where you are going, a trip out in one of these vehicles always feels like an event.

I have known these Range Rovers since they were announced at the end of 2001 (for a 2002 start to sales). At the time, I was the editor of *Land Rover Enthusiast* magazine, and, over the next few years, was able to sample several examples from Land Rover's press fleet as a result. I was particularly lucky to be invited to the launch of the TDV8 models in Spain, which I still think are the best of them all. So, I know how good these Range Rovers can be – and I also know how infuriatingly unreliable they can be if not properly maintained.

Quite a lot of the pictures in this book, by the way, have come from Land Rover, or Jaguar Land Rover as they have since become. Several others came from my own camera, and others were down to Nick Dimbleby, who is a friend, colleague, and fellow Range Rover nut. Many thanks to all who helped, either directly like this, or indirectly by telling me of their experiences with an L322.

... and the very last.

Contents

The Essential Buyer's Guide™ currency
At the time of publication a BG unit of currency "●" equals approximately
£1.00/US$1.27/Euro 1.12. Please adjust to suit current exchange rates.

1 Is it the right car for you?
– marriage guidance

Tall and short drivers
There is excellent headroom – even for tall drivers – and a wide range of seat adjustment also allows shorter drivers to find a suitable driving position. Even though the height-adjustable air suspension will lower the vehicle to aid access, some shorter drivers may find that side steps are a necessity.

Controls
The switchgear and auxiliary controls were deliberately designed to be easy to use and, as far as possible, intuitive. However, the high level of equipment, and similarly high level of configurability, means that it is advisable to spend some time getting familiar with the controls by reading the handbook. In many cases, once settings have been chosen, they can subsequently be ignored.

Will it fit in the garage?
An L322 Range Rover is 194.8in (4950mm) long, and 77in (1956mm) wide with the mirrors folded. At standard ride height, it stands 73.35in (1863mm) tall. You will probably have to fold the door mirrors in for most domestic garages, because otherwise the vehicle is 86.26in (2191mm) wide – that's more than seven feet!

The L322 Range Rover is a big car with an imposing presence. This is a very early example, with the headlights quite separate from the grille.

The 2006 models had a facelift. Clearly seen here is that the headlights were now cut into the grille, the front bumper was notched, and the side vents now had three slats instead of two.

Above & right: The supercharged models arrived for 2006, distinguished externally by a different grille and unique side vents. They also had a badge at the rear.

Satellite navigation is standard, and is seen here in a 2007-model Range Rover TDV8.

The overall interior ambience is that of a luxury car, as this early model demonstrates.

Interior space

These Range Rovers were designed to seat five people in a considerable degree of comfort. Rear legroom is excellent, even for the third (centre) passenger.

Luggage capacity

The load area will easily carry holiday luggage for four people. With the rear seat in use, the usable load area is 535 litres. Folding the rear seats down, of course, increases it so that extra-long loads can be carried. The rear seat also has a 60/40 split-fold design that increases the versatility of the load area.

The L322 configuration is 'classic' Range Rover – room for five adults inside, with a large boot accessed by a split tailgate.

Usability

Good acceleration and cruising speeds, plus excellent braking and manoeuvrability, make these Range Rovers good everyday vehicles. However, their size can sometimes prove to be a handicap, and may initially be daunting to some drivers.

The final facelift for 2010 brought yet another grille design, plus a 'three stripes' theme, seen here on the indicator lights and the side vent. It was also carried over to the tail lights.

Parts availability

Most items needed to keep one of these Range Rovers in running order are readily available. However, the parts unique to the special editions are in some cases difficult or impossible to obtain.

Plus points

The L322 Range Rover is an extremely spacious and comfortable vehicle that works well as a large family car. The 'command' driving position and good all-round visibility impart a feeling of security to the driver and passengers. The sheer size of the vehicle ensures that it has a presence, and it never looks out of place.

Minus points

The main drawbacks to these Range Rovers are their size, and the fact that they are not easily maintained on a DIY basis. This means that servicing and maintenance costs are likely to be high.

2 Cost considerations
– affordable, or a money pit?

An L322 Range Rover is not a vehicle that can be run on a shoestring budget. It is an expensive vehicle to own, and there is no way of reducing the bills except by neglecting it. Total neglect will quickly result in a vehicle that develops a rash of faults and becomes unusable.

You can choose to spend the money on regular and thorough maintenance, which should give you a reliable vehicle and peace of mind; or you can choose to spend the money reactively, waiting for something to go wrong because you haven't invested in preventive maintenance. One way or another, though, you will have to spend that money.

Servicing intervals
The manufacturer's recommendation is to have an L322 Range Rover serviced at least once a year, or every 15,000 miles. This is a minimum recommendation. All vehicles have a Service Interval Indicator (on the dashboard message screen) and in cases of hard use, this may flash up a warning message that a service is due early. The most important thing to remember is that the vehicle does need servicing regularly, and will deteriorate if it is not. A sheaf of papers proving that maintenance has been carried out to specification will also reassure potential buyers, if you ever decide to sell the vehicle.

A non-franchised specialist will typically charge around ●x165 to ●x175 for the minimum Oil Service. The more comprehensive A Service will be between ●x200 and ●x350 (the diesel models are more expensive), and the large or B Service will be between ●x300 and ●x400. Remember, though, that VAT will need to be added to these figures, and that your workshop may recommend attention to a multitude of additional items that are not on the standard servicing schedule. The cost of any additional parts needed, such as new brake pads, filters, and so on, will also be extra. So those bills can mount up.

Tax bands (UK)
In Britain, these Range Rovers belong in the higher bands for annual road tax (VED, or Vehicle Excise Duty). Typical figures at the time of writing were between ●x300 and ●x540 a year, depending on model.

Sample parts prices
Prices can vary considerably, and those shown here are typical. Generally speaking, Original Equipment (OE) items bought from Land Rover will be more expensive. Many pattern parts are available, but not all are made to OE standards. All prices are shown before VAT is added. Prices vary enormously (for exhausts, in particular); note that the best is not always the most expensive, but the cheapest is usually the worst value for money.

Air spring (front) ●x210

Alternator ●x160 (for Td6 diesel models)
●x190 (for 4.4 V8 and 4.2 supercharged models)

Brake pads ●x30 (single axle set)

Catalytic converter ●x250 (Td6 diesel)

Exhaust system ●x485 (petrol V8 to 2009, stainless steel back box and tail pipes)
●x500 (Td6 diesel, stainless steel)

Headlamp ●x275 (early models)
●x650 (Bi-Xenon, 2010 and later models)

Radiator ●x150

Shock absorber ●x120 (rear)
●x250 (damper and air spring assembly, front)

Tyre ●x125 upwards, depending on type and size

Wiper blade ●x15

Parts that are easy to find
Generally speaking, aftermarket suppliers can provide all of the consumable items needed to keep an L322 Range Rover in running order, although in some cases you may have to compromise on quality.

Parts that are hard to find
Most mechanical items are available, but in some cases the only source may be Land Rover, in which case the cost will be high.

3 Living with a Range Rover
– will you get along together?

The Range Rover L322 is an enormously impressive vehicle when everything is working as its manufacturers intended. Unfortunately, reliability is a long way from exemplary. Faults do develop over time, and if they are not attended to immediately, they may develop into bigger faults that will actually immobilise the vehicle rather than simply being an irritation. It has been said that the older these models become, the more they suit an enthusiast rather than an owner who wants everyday transport.

That said, servicing the vehicle as recommended by Land Rover, getting minor problems sorted out before they become major ones, and generally treating a Range Rover with respect, can lead to an enjoyable and rewarding ownership experience.

A lift-up top tailgate makes it easy to drop small items of shopping into the boot.

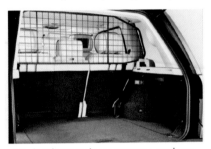

The load space is cavernous, and can be enlarged further by folding the rear seats forward. These have a one-third/two-thirds split for maximum flexibility. The spare wheel lives under the floor of the boot. Here, an accessory dog guard has been fitted.

The Td6 diesel engine was actually made by BMW, despite the Land Rover identification on the cosmetic cover panel. The German company knew it as the M57 engine.

Driving an L322 Range Rover is a quite special experience, and sometimes the vehicle feels a little too grand for just popping out to the shops. Like all Range Rovers, it features the 'Command Driving Position,' where the driver sits high up with a superb view all around the vehicle. Remarkably, this very large vehicle rarely feels as big as it really is, and the handling dynamics are quite superb for something of its size and weight. Nevertheless, in car parks or in other tight spots its true size does become apparent.

Performance ranges from very good to astonishingly impressive with one of the supercharged models. However, the supercharged models are the most expensive to run, and are not every owner's cup of tea. Despite what you may hear some people say, the Td6 diesel model is quite quick enough for everyday use and gives a good performance on motorways; it can also return about 25mpg, which is a bonus.

The more powerful TDV8 diesel is a pure delight, and in the real world is far and away the best of all the engine options. This engine delivers formidable acceleration thanks to its high torque at low speeds, and can return similar fuel figures to the earlier Td6 if used gently. If not, you will pay for your fun at the pumps.

There's more information about the various petrol engines in Chapter 4, but, for the moment, let's just say that with any of the non-supercharged V8s, you will struggle to better 18-20mpg on a regular basis. (Note that these engines were not sold in Britain after 2008). If you choose one of the Supercharged models, don't expect much better than 15-16mpg from normal use, and look forward to some really upsetting figures if you enjoy using the vehicle hard.

With all engine types, the permanent four-wheel drive provides fuss-free traction and roadholding in the wet, plus the ability to press on through snow if necessary. All L322 Range Rovers also have a highly sophisticated all-independent air suspension system that delivers a remarkably smooth ride. A clever electronic control system allows this to give the vehicle quite awesome off-road ability in all kinds of tricky terrain (more on this in a minute); on the 2006 and later models, another electronic system – called 'Terrain Response' – optimises the Range Rover's traction and dynamic systems to make life easy for the driver.

Realistically, the diesel models are best for everyday use in Britain and Europe.

There is an entirely different top cover for the 4.2-litre supercharged V8 petrol engine.

The early 4.4-litre V8 engine was also made by BMW, and was known by their M62 designation. Like the Td6, its cosmetic top cover was given Land Rover branding.

The TDV8 engine was only ever used in Land Rover products, and is probably the best of all the engines in the L322 range.

The 5.0-litre V8 engines were known as LR-V8 types. This is the supercharged version – little of the engine itself is actually visible.

The eight raised silver sections of the cosmetic cover represent the eight cylinders of the 4.4-litre Jaguar-derived V8 engine.

Fuel economy is possible, and this figure was displayed on the dashboard of a 2009-model TDV8 – but you would be unwise to expect to see such figures very often!

The L322 Range Rover is a highly capable off-road vehicle, as much at home in conditions like these as it is at speed on a motorway.

Does the L322 Range Rover qualify as a classic car? There is no doubt that it will become appreciated as a classic of its kind in the future, but it's worth saying here and now that if your idea of classic car ownership involves a lot of tinkering with a spanner, an L322 is not for you. It was designed for wealthy owners who could afford to have it regularly maintained by a Land Rover dealership, and not for servicing at home. An absolute minimum requirement for working on one of these is a special electronic diagnostics kit – plus large amounts of patience, of course. Things do go wrong, typically with the complex electronic systems, and owner maintenance can be very frustrating and time-consuming.

Basic maintenance, such as oil and brake pad changes, are obviously within the scope of the keen DIY owner, but, beyond that, you have to be honest with yourself about your competence and enthusiasm. A good compromise is to do as much as possible of the routine maintenance yourself, but to find a local independent specialist who will help you out when you run into difficulties, or take on the more difficult jobs for you.

The question of off-road use has already been raised, and you should know that an L322 Range Rover has rough-terrain abilities that exceed the courage of many owners. However, it is also true that relatively few owners have taken to using these vehicles regularly at off-road play days and the like. The reason is quite simple: the vehicle can cope, but if the driver makes a mistake and damages it, there will be a big bill. It is not at all the same as bending the panels on an early Land Rover and then hammering them out in the garage at the weekend!

4 Relative values
– which model for you?

Although the overall shape of the L322 Range Rover did not change in ten years of production, there were two face-lifts. The first came in Autumn 2005, when a two-bar mesh grille replaced the original plastic grille vanes. The second was in Autumn 2009, which brought a new, three-element grille, with revised lights front and rear that incorporated triple horizontal elements to match the grille. There were several changes of alloy wheel design over the years.

The first L322s had a 4.4-litre V8 petrol engine with 282bhp or a 3.0-litre 'Td6' turbocharged diesel with 174bhp. Both were manufactured by BMW. The V8 is relatively uncommon in Europe, but was the only engine available in the USA. From Summer 2005, the V8 petrol engine gave way to two new engines, of Jaguar origin. These were a 306bhp 4.4-litre V8 and a 390bhp 4.2-litre supercharged V8. This round of changes was completed a year later when a new 268bhp TDV8 diesel replaced the Td6.

The TDV8 engine is highly admired and in demand, so expect the prices of these models to be quite high.

The naturally-aspirated V8 was withdrawn from sale in Europe in Autumn 2007 (but remained available elsewhere). A second round of engine changes began in Summer 2009, when 5.0-litre Jaguar-derived V8s replaced the older two, with 375bhp in naturally-aspirated form and 510bhp in supercharged form. A year later, the TDV8 was enlarged to 4.4 litres and now delivered 308bhp.

The standard Land Rover badge is the green oval ...

... but the supercharged L322 models had a black oval. Some owners have replaced the original green oval with a black one; some have gone even further in their attempt to make a lower specification model look like one of the supercharged models.

Autobiography is the highest equipment level that was in standard production. But do you really need all the extras it brings, and are you really prepared to pay extra for them?

Gearboxes were invariably automatic, and all models came with very high levels of standard equipment. Designations changed over the years, but SE denotes an entry-level model, while HSE is next up, and Vogue is above that. Vogue SE goes one higher and, towards the end of production, Autobiography became the top level. There were also special editions, which varied from one country to another. In Britain, they included the Autobiography Edition (2003) and the 35th Anniversary Edition (2005). These had combinations of features not available elsewhere.

There is always a strong demand for Supercharged models, which tends to keep prices up. Many buyers favour the TDV8 diesel, so again strong demand means high prices. Most affordable are likely to be Td6 models. Some people claim these are under-powered, but in fact they have as much performance as you need for ordinary everyday use. Special editions are rare – but whether you are prepared to pay extra for that rarity is your decision.

One of the most attractive of all L322 models was the 35th Anniversary edition from 2005 (the original Range Rover was introduced in 1970). Examples of this are already being salted away by Range Rover enthusiasts – but if you intend to use your L322 every day, the typically high asking price of one of these is hard to justify.

5 Before you view
– be well informed

To avoid a wasted journey, and the disappointment of finding that the Range Rover does not match your expectations, it will help if you're very clear about what questions you want to ask before you pick up the telephone. Some of these points might appear basic but when you're excited about the prospect of buying your dream classic, it's amazing how some of the most obvious things slip the mind ... Also check the current values of the model you are interested in in classic car magazines, which give both a price guide and auction results.

Where is the car?
Is it going to be worth travelling to the next county/state, or even across a border? A locally advertised car, although it may not sound very interesting, can add to your knowledge for very little effort, so make a visit – it might even be in better condition than expected.

Dealer or private sale
Establish early on if the car is being sold by its owner or by a trader. A private owner should have all the history, so don't be afraid to ask detailed questions. A dealer may have more limited knowledge of a car's history, but should have some documentation. A dealer may offer a warranty/guarantee (ask for a printed copy) and finance.

Cost of collection and delivery
A dealer may well be used to quoting for delivery by car transporter. A private owner may agree to meet you halfway, but only agree to this after you have seen the car at the vendor's address to validate the documents. Conversely, you could meet halfway and agree the sale but insist on meeting at the vendor's address for the handover.

View – when and where
It is always preferable to view at the vendor's home or business premises. In the case of a private sale, the car's documentation should tally with the vendor's name and address. Arrange to view only in daylight and avoid a wet day. Most cars look better in poor light or when wet.

Reason for sale
Do make it one of the first questions. Why is the car being sold and how long has it been with the current owner? How many previous owners?

Aftermarket 'specials'
A number of highly reputable aftermarket specialists offered high-performance conversions of the L322 Range Rover, such as Overfinch in Britain and Arden in Germany. These conversions were few and far between, mainly because of their cost, and you are unlikely to find many (if any) for sale. They have a special interest to hard-core enthusiasts but you should be aware that they are likely to need special maintenance as well.

A few specialist aftermarket companies offered bespoke conversions of the L322 Range Rover. In Germany, Hamann had its HM 5.0 conversion from early on, with its own 5.0-litre derivative of the BMW V8 engine. Vehicles like this are very uncommon and are likely to be pricey if they come up for sale.

Condition (body/chassis/interior/mechanicals)

Ask for an honest appraisal of the car's condition. Ask specifically about some of the check items described in Chapter 7.

All original specification

An original equipment car is invariably of higher value than a customised version.

Matching data/legal ownership

Do VIN/chassis, engine numbers and licence plate match the official registration document? Is the owner's name and address recorded in the official registration documents?

For those countries that require an annual test of roadworthiness, does the car have a document showing it complies (an MOT certificate in the UK, which can be verified on 0845 600 5977)?

If a smog/emissions certificate is mandatory, does the car have one?

If required, does the car carry a current road fund licence/licence plate tag?

Does the vendor own the car outright? Money might be owed to a finance company or bank – the car could even be stolen. Several organisations will supply the data on ownership, based on the car's licence plate number, for a fee. Such companies can often also tell you whether the car has been 'written-off' by an insurance company.

In the UK these organisations can supply vehicle data:

HPI – 01722 422 422
AA – 0870 600 0836
DVLA – 0870 240 0010
RAC – 0870 533 3660
Other countries will have similar organisations.

Unleaded fuel
All petrol-engined L322 Range Rovers were designed to run on unleaded fuel and came with catalytic converters as standard.

Insurance
Check with your existing insurer before setting out; your current policy might not cover you to drive the car if you do purchase it.

How you can pay
A cheque will take several days to clear and the seller may prefer to sell to a cash buyer. However, a banker's draft (a cheque issued by a bank) is as good as cash, but safer, so contact your own bank and become familiar with the formalities that are necessary to obtain one.

Buying at auction?
If the intention is to buy at auction, see Chapter 10 for further advice.

Professional vehicle check (mechanical examination)
There are often marque/model specialists who will undertake professional examination of a vehicle on your behalf. Owners' clubs will be able to put you in touch with such specialists.

Other organisations that will carry out a general professional check in the UK are:
AA – 0800 085 3007 (motoring organisation with vehicle inspectors)
ABS – 0800 358 5855 (specialist vehicle inspection company)
RAC – 0870 533 3660 (motoring organisation with vehicle inspectors)
Other countries will have similar organisations.

The wheels, the paint and the bodykit are the most obvious enhancements on this Overfinch L322. Examples like this are very rare and will be priced accordingly if they come onto the market; are they worth the extra to you?

6 Inspection equipment
– these items will really help

This book
Reading glasses (if you need them for close work)
Magnet (not powerful, a fridge magnet is ideal)
Torch
Probe (a small screwdriver works very well)
Overalls
Mirror on a stick
Digital camera
A friend, preferably a knowledgeable enthusiast

Before you rush out the door, gather together a few items that will help as you work your way around the Range Rover. This book is designed to be your guide at every step, so take it along and use the check boxes to help you assess each area of the car you're interested in. Don't be afraid to let the seller see you using it.

Take your reading glasses if you need them to read documents and make close up inspections.

A magnet will help you check if the car is full of filler, and you can use it to sample bodywork areas all around the car, always taking care, of course, not to damage the paintwork. However, bear in mind that many of the Range Rover's outer panels are made of aluminium (see Chapter 7); do not get carried away and assume that apparently non-magnetic panels are full of filler.

A torch with fresh batteries will be useful for peering into the wheelarches and under the vehicle.

A small screwdriver can be used - with care - as a probe, particularly in the wheelarches and on the underside. With this you should be able to check an area of severe corrosion, but be careful - if it's really bad the screwdriver might go right through the metal!

Be prepared to get dirty. Take along a pair of overalls, if you have them. Fixing a mirror at an angle on the end of a stick may seem odd, but you'll probably need it to check the condition of the underside of the vehicle. It will also help you to peer into some of the important crevices. You can also use it, together with the torch, along the underside of the sills and on the floor.

If you have the use of a digital camera, take it along so that later you can study some areas of the car more closely. Take a picture of any part of the car that causes you concern, and seek a friend's opinion.

Ideally, have a friend or knowledgeable enthusiast accompany you: a second opinion is always valuable.

7 Fifteen minute evaluation
– walk away or stay?

At this stage of the game, you're looking only for the major problems that might put you off buying a particular vehicle. They are not the only problems that show up – and you may spot other, less worrisome problems while you're looking for these – but they are the ones that are most expensive to put right.

An L322 Range Rover can only be expected to give its best if its owners do the same, especially when it comes to regular maintenance. So, for that reason, the top priority when examining a vehicle for sale is to take a look at the service history. If there is none, your best advice is to walk away, so it's advisable to save everybody's time and patience by asking about the history in advance over the phone. There should be a collection of invoices, and there should be a number of stamps in the vehicle's service book. The size of some of the invoices might frighten you, but you can be reassured that somebody else has paid to have the work done so that you won't have to.

There should also be an owner's handbook, which is quite a thick volume that explains how to operate the onboard equipment, of which there is a lot. Make sure that it is the right handbook for the vehicle, because specifications did change over the years. This book will become a good friend to you if you do eventually buy the vehicle, and it is important to read it. You would be surprised how many questions come up on owners' internet forums that could be answered by a look in the handbook.

Exterior
The next thing to do is to make a visual inspection of the vehicle, looking for scrapes and dents in the panels that will suggest the owner has not been too careful with it. In particular, look at the corners of the bumper aprons and at the wheelarches, which are vulnerable to damage simply because this is a big vehicle and its extremities are not always easy to see from the driving seat. You would expect the owner of such a large and prestigious vehicle to take reasonable care of it, and bodywork in poor condition can be a warning sign that other areas of the Range Rover's welfare have been neglected.

The L322 is a large vehicle, and corners often get scraped – sometimes without the owner realising it until later.

Take a look at the wheels and tyres, too. There should be plenty of tread on the tyres, and no signs of inconsistent wear: a new set of tyres will be expensive, and odd wear points to something being out of alignment in the suspension or steering. Check for scuffing of the alloy wheels, which is usually caused by contact with a kerb. The more scuffing there is, the less careful the owner has been with the vehicle.

Low-profile tyres are more vulnerable to sidewall damage and tend to be more expensive to replace than others; they also offer the wheels less protection against kerbing damage. Land Rover offered wheel sizes of between 18 and 21 inches, and went no larger because the bigger, ultra-low-profile tyres are extremely vulnerable to damage on a Range Rover. Beware, then, of aftermarket 22-inch wheels.

Check the alloy wheels for signs of kerbing damage. This one is on a 2010 model, and shows the branded brake callipers used on late examples.

Interior

Try not to let the opulence of the passenger cabin overwhelm you if this is the first time you've examined an L322. Leather is standard, as are power-adjusted seats, and the whole cabin feels extremely spacious. But do look carefully for some of the obvious problems, such as worn or damaged leather. Another common problem is a broken plastic finisher on the outer edge of the driver's seat cushion. This can be caused if a heavy driver has used the vehicle a little roughly. More detailed checks can be saved for a thorough examination of the vehicle later.

The passenger cabin is quite opulent, as befits a luxury car. The two-tone upholstery was used for the Autobiography models.

Electrical system

The electrical system is hidden and out of sight, and for that reason it is all too easy to ignore it when looking at an L322 for sale. However, the truth is that electrical gremlins are a very major factor in the condition and viability of these vehicles, because so much of the onboard equipment is electrically powered. The problems with the electrical system can range from annoying little ones to major functional faults, which can be expensive to put right.

As electrics are so fundamental to the L322's existence, the first thing to check is the battery. A worn-out battery that will not hold its charge

There were several different control layouts. These paddle switches are on an early model; the yellow one is for Hill Descent Control and the white one for range selection in the transfer box.

This is a 2007 model. The rotary knob selects the Terrain Response settings, and the transfer box range selector is on the right at the rear, with HDC in the middle and suspension height adjustment on the left.

In the final models (this one is from 2011), there is a rotary control for the primary gearbox; the Terrain Response settings are selected by a rocker switch, but the HDC, transfer box, and suspension switches at the back of the console are as before.

is bound to cause problems: when sensors in the system detect that the current flowing to certain items is lower than ideal, they will flag up a warning on the driver's message board. Also very important is that the alternator is in tip-top condition, because if it fails to keep the battery fully charged, the same symptoms will appear. Ask how old the battery is, and look for proof in the vehicle's paperwork. Watch out during your test-drive for warning messages that appear and disappear on the message panel.

When you switch the ignition on, all of the dashboard warning lights should come on, and should then go

This cutaway display transmission assembly shows the automatic gearbox (with torque converter visible at the front), and the transfer gearbox, with its chain drive on display.

out again very soon after the engine has started. There are two things to watch out for here. One is that all of the warning lights actually do come on in the first place, because it is not unknown for unscrupulous sellers to remove a warning light bulb in order to disguise a fault. The other thing to check is that they all go out: only the handbrake warning light should stay on (assuming the handbrake is on). Any others that remain illuminated are flagging up faults that will need further investigation.

It will take you a long time to check that all of the onboard electrical items are correctly functioning, and you can safely put off that thorough check until you come back for a second look at the vehicle – if you do decide to do so. Even so, during this first brief encounter, it's advisable to run through the basics. Does the central locking work correctly? Do all the windows rise and drop as they should? What about the door mirror adjustment? And, finally, make sure that the front seat adjustment is in order. There are several electric motors involved here, and they can, and do, fail (often seizing from lack of use). The driver's seat is more likely to be affected, but it is worth checking the adjustment of the passenger's front seat as well.

Engine

There is not a lot to see of any of the engines in the L322 Range Rover. In each case, a cosmetic plastic cover conceals the hardware from view, and many owners have suggested that Land Rover designed the vehicle to discourage DIY-minded owners from having a go at their own maintenance. At this stage, look only for the more obvious engine faults, such as poor starting, rough running, or overheating. A visual check for oil and coolant leaks is also worthwhile, but a more detailed appraisal of the engine can wait until you come back for a second and more detailed look at the vehicle – if you do.

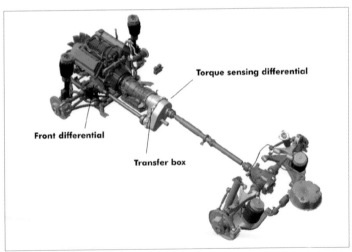

It helps when looking at a vehicle to have some idea of how it is laid out! This is the transmission system of the L322, showing clearly how the drive is taken to the front wheels from the transfer gearbox.

Gearboxes

All L322 models have an automatic primary gearbox and a two-speed transfer gearbox. The transfer gearbox divides the drive between the front and rear pairs of wheels, and also gives access to low range – which gives a full set of lower gear ratios for low-speed and off-road work.

You should pay special attention to the primary gearbox. The later six-speed and, on the TDV8, eight-speed types give relatively little trouble. However, the early five-speed types were notoriously troublesome, largely because they were near the limit of their torque capacity behind the Range Rover's engines.

There are two types of five-speed gearbox: the one used with the petrol engines being manufactured by ZF, and the one used with the Td6 diesel engine, originating with General Motors in Strasbourg. It is the GM gearbox that is the most problematic, but, in fairness, the ZF does not lag far behind. Find out first whether the gearbox has ever been changed: many were replaced under warranty, although unfortunately there is no guarantee that the replacement unit was any better than the original.

What you do need to know, however, is how many miles the vehicle has done on its current gearbox. This is because gearbox failure becomes more likely as the miles mount up. Above 60,000 miles is the danger zone. Ask the owner if the gearbox oil and filter have ever been changed. If they have, it's a sign that somebody has tried to treat the gearbox with respect. These gearboxes were theoretically sealed for life and needed no top-ups – but changing the oil at sensible intervals can certainly prolong their life.

When driving the vehicle, abrupt or reluctant gear changes should alert you to an impending problem. Warning lights or messages on the dashboard will confirm if there is trouble ahead. A new gearbox can be very expensive; think in the region of ●x5000, although by hunting around you can find specialists who can rebuild them for a cheaper cost.

While checking that all is well with the main gearbox, it is always sensible to make sure that the transfer gearbox's low range does engage properly and that the vehicle will drive in low range (which can be useful for low-speed towing manoeuvres as well as in off-road driving). Selection is by a switch at the rear of the centre console, and it is not unknown for the servo motor that does the actual work to seize up if it has not been used much. Replacements are expensive. At the same time, test the Hill Descent Control (operated by another switch on the console), which limits downhill speed in off-road conditions by pulsing the brakes.

Front differential

There was never a problem with the front differential on the L322, although it is quite commonplace to hear people talking about a problem in this area as affecting the differential. The reality is that, on pre-2006 models, the front drive shafts could go out of alignment and fail, leaving the Range Rover with no drive to the front wheels.

In most cases, the problem will have been rectified by a recall action, under which dealers fitted new driveshafts that contained a flexible joint to absorb the movement that was causing the damage. If you're looking at an early Range Rover, check the service history to see that this has been done. Listen while driving the vehicle for a knocking noise at low speed on full steering lock – a fairly reliable indicator that the problem has not been completely solved.

Suspension

The Range Rover's superb ride is achieved by means of air suspension. This means that, in effect, each corner of the vehicle rides on a column of air instead of a steel spring. The air suspension has a complex electronic control system that will lower the vehicle automatically to improve stability (and reduce aerodynamic drag) at speeds of over 60mph, and can lower the vehicle under the driver's control to make entry and exit easier. This suspension can also raise the Range Rover, again under the driver's control, to clear obstacles during off-road driving or for wading. Clever electronics ensure that the all-independent suspension behaves like the live-axled system in earlier Range Rovers during off-road use, to give maximum traction.

The front suspension is carried on a subframe. This view shows the air springs very clearly.

In normal use, the system is entirely unobtrusive. Unfortunately, it is also prone to failures, and it is very important to check for correct functioning during your first evaluation of any Range Rover. Use the selector on the console behind the gear selector to run through the height settings. The vehicle should rise or fall quickly, smoothly, and without making protesting noises. If it does not, there is a problem with a component within the electrical control system.

The usual suspect if the air suspension misbehaves is the air compressor, which is located under the boot floor in the spare wheel well. It may be affected by water, but the most common cause of failure is a leak in the system. Sensors detect when more air is needed in the air springs, and trigger the compressor to provide that air. If there is a leak, the correct air pressure may not be obtained and the compressor will continue to run, eventually burning itself out. Listen, then, for noise from the compressor.

Leaks are most commonly associated with the air springs themselves, which are consumable items that have to be replaced every few years. In essence, they are large rubber bags, and the constant flexing that they endure eventually wears the rubber and creates holes in it. Check each bag for signs of splitting and cracking, especially at the lower end, and remember that air leaks can seem to be intermittent because the rubber can sometimes fold over a pinhole leak and temporarily stop or reduce it.

Underneath

You can learn more about the way a vehicle has been treated by getting underneath it and taking a good look at the underside. The L322 Range Rover does not have a separate chassis but is a monocoque construction, which, in crude terms, means that the body is just one big box to which everything else is bolted.

However, there are strengthening pressings on the underside of the body that create the rigidity necessary for refinement and good handling. There are also

The underlying structure of the bodyshell is steel, and this view shows how the rear wings are part of that structure.

sub-frames. Take a look at all these to check for scrapes and dents, which is the type of damage that a vehicle may sustain in off-road use. Really bad damage may continue on to the underside of the floorpans as well. From this examination, you will discover not only whether the Range Rover has had much off-road use, but also how carefully its driver treated it in those conditions. You can draw some useful conclusions from this knowledge.

Don't forget to also check the ground under the vehicle for oil stains or other indications of fluid leaks. You can save a more detailed inspection for later – if you do go back for a second look.

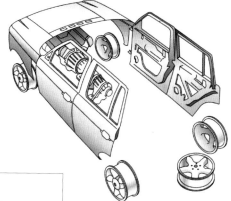

Aluminium alloy is used extensively, to save weight. Door panels, front wings and bonnet are all made of alloy, as are the wheels, transmission casings, and BMW V8 engine shown here.

The instrument panel is capable of conveying a great deal of information to the driver, as this drawing reveals. At this stage, you only need to check the basic functions.

8 Key points
– where to look for problems

After you've been for a first look at an L322 that's for sale, you'll want to spend some time thinking over what you've seen and deciding whether to go for a second look, which is what the next chapter is all about.

Thinking it over means sorting out the potentially confusing mass of information that you've just gathered so that you can make some sense of it. Begin by focussing on some fundamental questions:

* Is the Range Rover structurally sound?
* Is it cosmetically acceptable?
* Does the engine seem good?

There are multiple different specifications for the L322, so think very carefully about whether the one you've seen is the one you want. Pictured here is an early Autobiography model; later rear lights were different.

Some of the early wheel designs were a little uninspired, but some people find the later ones rather fussy. This is one of those late designs. Wheels can always be changed, but a full set of wheels and tyres is expensive!

If the answers to all three of those questions are 'yes,' you're probably going to want to go back for that second look. If you answer 'no' to any of them, you're probably going to be better off giving this one a miss.

Still tempted? All right then, here are three more deal-breaker questions:

* How much work will you have to do to it to make it meet your standards?
* Is it really the L322 you want? For example, is it an early BMW-engined model when you really wanted a late one with a Ford-Jaguar engine?
* Are you going to have to do some tricky explaining to your wife/husband/ significant other when you get it home?

If you've been honest in your answers to these questions, and you still think you might buy the vehicle, move on to the next chapter.

The frontal appearance changed over the years. This is a 2012 model, with the late style of bodykit.

Dashboards changed quite a lot, too. This is on a 2008 Autobiography model, with the dark wood finishers; the lighter wood changes the appearance quite considerably.

9 Serious evaluation
– 60 minutes for years of enjoyment

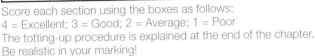

Score each section using the boxes as follows:
4 = Excellent; 3 = Good; 2 = Average; 1 = Poor
The totting-up procedure is explained at the end of the chapter.
Be realistic in your marking!

The best way to use this section is to tick the boxes as you go along, because you won't be able to remember all the details of the vehicle when you sit down to think about it later on. The inspection sequence follows a logical order, so you'll start with the outside of the vehicle, check the underside, move on to the interior, and then examine the engine bay. But first of all, we think it's sensible to take a test drive. This will highlight a number of things that you can check later, when you return from the drive, and that a simple visual inspection probably would not have revealed.

Pre-inspection diagnostic check

If you're quite serious about the Range Rover you're going to see, it's never a bad idea to get a local specialist to visit the vehicle and put it through a diagnostic test on specialist equipment. Ask the owner's permission first, of course! A clean bill of health takes much of the risk out of buying one of these models, and of course a negative report may put you off buying the vehicle altogether – or may give you some bargaining power when it comes to haggling over a price. Most specialists will charge about ●x50 for this service – which is peanuts compared to the money and trouble a diagnostic check might save you.

In an ideal world, you would have the diagnostic check done twice, the second time after driving the vehicle, because faults 'cleared' in the first check might well show up again. Realistically, though, a single check will be enough as long as you ask for a full list of the fault codes that appeared, whether cleared or not. The codes typically appear as numbers, but you can find decoding lists on the web to help you work out what they mean.

At this stage of the game, you really need to drive the Range Rover you're assessing and make a mental note of anything that doesn't seem quite right.

Test drive

With the L322 Range Rover, it makes good sense to take the vehicle for a run early on in your evaluation. This is because the test drive may draw attention to a number of things that you really want to check afterwards. So the first thing to do is to double-check the position on insurance: not every insurance policy covers you for using somebody else's vehicle. Also worth checking is that the vehicle itself is road legal: if you take a test drive on a public road in a vehicle without a valid roadworthiness certificate, you will be breaking the law.

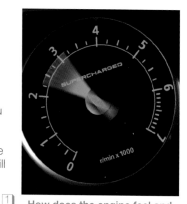

How does the engine feel and sound? If it's a supercharged example, response to the accelerator should be instantaneous – and exciting.

Messages and warning lights 4 3 2 1

As you turn the ignition key, a series of dashboard lights should come on, and the vehicle will perform its own systems checks. Most lights will go out of their own accord when the engine starts, although obviously the handbrake light will not if the handbrake is on. Look out for lights that don't go out, and make a mental note of which ones they are. It's possible that some will go out once the vehicle starts moving, but it's also possible that some won't go out at all. Those are the ones for the systems you'll want to double-check later.

Keep an eye on the message centre, too. A 'door open' warning when all doors are firmly shut is annoying rather than critical, but it does indicate that there is a fault that will need attention. Other messages – and there are too many possibilities to list them all here – should not be ignored. It's always worth asking the owner (who will almost certainly be in the vehicle with you) whether he or she has tried to deal with the problem that a message indicates. The response might give you valuable insight into how well the Range Rover has been looked after.

The steering column is adjustable for height and reach, in each case by means of electric servo motors. Motors that haven't been used for some time (such as when only one driver has used the vehicle over a number of years) may seize. A seized steering column adjustment is a negotiating point when it comes to the price.

Ride and handling 4 3 2 1

The air suspension should give a very smooth ride, although with the larger wheel sizes that smoothness can deteriorate. Although you'll feel major bumps through the seat of your pants, there should not be any serious jarring. If there is, make a mental note to check the air springs and maybe the bushes as well. The steering should feel fairly direct and accurate, but don't expect to be able to throw a vehicle of this size around as if it's a sports car. No engineering, however good, has yet overcome the laws of physics.

If the steering seems graunchy or notchy when you turn the wheel, the cause may be a low level of power steering fluid or a slipping auxiliary drivebelt that drives the PAS pump. This is something else to check for later.

Engine health and performance 4 3 2 1

How does the engine feel? How does it sound? Expect smooth acceleration from all the engines that were offered in the L322, and listen carefully for odd noises, such as the rattle of a worn supercharger on models that have one, or the irregular tinkling or pinging noise that might suggest a misfire.

Gearbox

Check how the automatic gearbox performs. Are there clunks when a gear is selected from rest? If so, there's probably wear in the propshaft joints. Is the box reluctant to change up and down, or are the changes jerky? Remember that gearbox wear has always been a problem in the L322. Remember, too, that early models suffered from front driveshaft problems, which may well reveal themselves as a knocking noise on full steering lock at low speeds, such as when manoeuvring in a car park.

Check that the servo motor assisting selection of low range in the transfer box works properly. This is another one of those items that can seize up through lack of use. You may have no plans to use the Range Rover off-road, but you can use a problem here as a negotiating point when it comes to agreeing a price.

Brakes

There's no need to stand the vehicle on its nose deliberately; normal driving will probably give you more than one opportunity to stamp on the brakes and see whether they pull to one side or halt the vehicle in a straight line. Look out for vibration from the discs, which do wear out on a heavy vehicle like this one. If the brakes are not 100% reassuring, you need to find out why.

On later models with the electronic handbrake, make sure that the handbrake does self-release as the vehicle moves off. A hill start gives you a good opportunity to apply the handbrake and then see if it behaves properly in these circumstances.

Heating and air-conditioning

The L322 has a complex and sophisticated heating and air-conditioning system, but the driver interface is very simple: you set the cabin temperature you want and then allow the system to achieve it. It's very easy to ignore, but also easy to test during a test drive. Does the heater work properly? If it's deficient on a diesel model, suspect a water pump problem. This will need attention right away as it can lead to overheating of the engine; you might wonder why the present owner hasn't already done something about it.

Does the air-conditioning cool the cabin down quickly? If not, there's a problem.

Exterior

Back at the vendor's place, you can begin your series of other checks as the Range Rover cools down. It makes sense to begin with the outside of the vehicle.

Paintwork

Most of the paint options for the L322 Range Rover were metallic or micatallic types, which are notoriously difficult to touch-in seamlessly after a scrape. The quality of the original paintwork was very high, so be suspicious of paint that seems to have dulled or become crazed over the years. If there are paint problems, use them as a bargaining point – and be prepared for a large bill to put it right if you decide to buy the vehicle.

If there is evidence of repainting, try to find out why the work was done. Was the vehicle involved in a collision? If so, this should alert you to look for other signs of damage that may be less visible. Expect to find a few stone chips on the leading edge of the bonnet

Rust hasn't been a major problem on the L322, but there are some weak spots. Here's one, at the back of the rear wheelarch.

Here's another regular rust spot, just above the plastic bumper behind the wheelarch. The rear wings are steel, of course, not alloy.

It's also worth checking the leading edge of each rear wheelarch, with the door open.

Although the L322 Range Rover has a monocoque structure, there are some strong underfloor members that look very much like traditional chassis rails. Here they are in yellow, on a specially prepared cutaway demonstration model that was made in Australia.

The strong underfloor members at the rear can be seen in this second picture of the Australian cutaway. It was quite old when photographed, and rust had begun to attack the outer wing panel where it had been cut – a reminder that these wings are steel!

and, as you'll have spotted in your preliminary evaluation, a few minor scrapes on the corners of the front bumper or the wheel arches, and maybe on the rear bumper as well.

Body panels and structure

Panel fit on these vehicles benefited from BMW's input to the Land Rover assembly process, and was as good as that found on more conventional luxury cars of the time. For that reason, you should be very suspicious of any misaligned or poor-fitting panels. They are likely to be an indicator of replacement work, and you need to discover why. Chances are, the vehicle has been involved in an accident at some time.

Similarly, signs of corrosion in body panels (note that many are aluminium) usually indicate poor-quality repair work. Again, try to find out why the repair was necessary in the first place.

Monocoque

The steel monocoque frame at the heart of these Range Rovers should be rust-free. If it isn't, it has almost certainly been poorly repaired after accident damage. Having said that, one exposed area of the monocoque does suffer from rust, and that is the forward edges of the rear wheelarches, which are exposed when the rear doors are open. It is a rare L322 that does not have some sign of rust here, but it is not normally a major problem. Make a note to get it repaired sooner rather than later.

Doors and tailgate

The Range Rover's doors are panelled in aluminium alloy, which is resistant to corrosion but can become dented through rough usage. It goes without saying that all four doors should fit extremely well; the spectre of variable panel gaps that haunted the first-generation Range Rover had been banished by the time these were being built. So, if there are uneven gaps, be suspicious. Look for poor fit of the lower door cladding, too, because uneven gaps between this and the aluminium alloy door panel suggest that the latter has been distorted and subsequently repaired.

Make sure the central locking locks and unlocks all the doors and the tailgate, because electrical problems are relatively common on these Range Rovers. Check the bottom edge of the lower tailgate for rust. Bizarrely, these tailgates can also be damaged by people sitting on them.

The lower tailgate is prone both to damage and to rust. Open it to check the sides as well as the more visible areas.

Roof panel & sunroof

The roof panel itself will not normally have any problems, but many owners never look at or clean the roof of a Range Rover from the time they buy it, and that can lead to cosmetic problems. The first sign of neglect is when the clear varnish over the paint starts to peel off. More serious damage may be caused during the fitting or removal of a roof rack.

It is not unknown for the roof seams to leak, allowing water to run into the body and create havoc with any electrical system in its path. All models have an electrically operated sunroof, and you should make sure that this will actually open and close properly. Sunroofs can seize through lack of use, and the electric motor can burn out if the roof itself has seized. Sunroofs can also develop leaks, although this is far less of a problem on the L322 than on other Land Rover models.

Checking under the car

If you're going to be really thorough with your inspection, you need to spread out a blanket or similar on the ground, and crawl under the vehicle to take a closer look. A torch will certainly help you see into areas that are normally hidden from view. Better still, if you're examining the vehicle in a garage workshop, ask to have the vehicle lifted up on a hoist. Or, if the seller has an inspection pit, ask if the vehicle can be driven over that pit so that you can inspect it from underneath. But be warned: many pits collect water, so you may find yourself wading!

Oil and fluid leaks

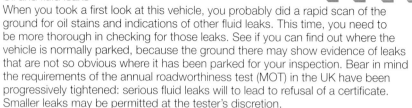

When you took a first look at this vehicle, you probably did a rapid scan of the ground for oil stains and indications of other fluid leaks. This time, you need to be more thorough in checking for those leaks. See if you can find out where the vehicle is normally parked, because the ground there may show evidence of leaks that are not so obvious where it has been parked for your inspection. Bear in mind the requirements of the annual roadworthiness test (MOT) in the UK have been progressively tightened: serious fluid leaks will to lead to refusal of a certificate. Smaller leaks may be permitted at the tester's discretion.

If you find evidence of leaks, see if you can find where the fluid is coming from. The more obvious leaks may be of engine oil, and this will typically come from the sump. Oil leaks may also come from differential drain plugs that are not sealing properly. Differential casings and gearboxes are fairly well protected, but do check them for cracked casings on a Range Rover that has been used a lot off-road. That sort of damage is going to be expensive to fix.

There may also be leaks from the power steering system, either from the hydraulic pipes or from the steering rack. Land Rover recommended a special cold climate fluid for the system, which is not only expensive but also clear, rather than red like many other types of PAS fluid. So don't assume that only red fluid will indicate a power steering leak.

Structure

You checked underneath the Range Rover for signs of structural damage on your first examination. If you're still happy, then all's well and good. But if there were areas you wanted to check again, now's the time to do so. In particular, check for any signs of rippling in the underframe pressings that might have been caused by a collision.

Suspension

You checked for the most obvious faults with the air suspension when you gave the vehicle that initial examination. If you had any doubts at that stage, now is the time to deal with them. Run through the height control settings again, check for error messages on the dashboard, and listen for odd noises from the compressor.

You can go a step further in your checks now. It's quite common to hear a rattle from the front suspension when driving over a rough surface, and even to feel an accompanying twitch through the steering wheel. Unfortunately, it isn't easy to investigate this problem. Even if you test all the bushes with a bar, and even if you jack the vehicle up to look for play, you might not find any. To do the job properly, you will need the vehicle on a hoist, and to look for excessive movement in the bushes and ball joints while somebody rocks the steering wheel from side to side. The culprit is usually the front suspension lower ball joint, but it is easier to replace the whole suspension arm than to deal with the ball joint on its own. A secondary problem at the front end is a light rattle over rough surfaces, and the cause of that is, typically, worn bushes in the suspension drop links.

When driving the vehicle, were there any odd clonks from the rear suspension as it passed over bumps? If so, there's a good chance that the rear hub bushes are on the way out; these are the ones between the hubs and the wishbones, and they eventually perish and lose their effectiveness. The bushes are not easily replaced as a DIY job, because you need a special tool to push the old bushes out.

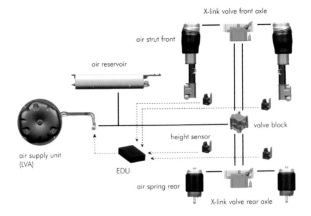

X-link valve front axle

air strut front

air reservoir

valve block

height sensor

air supply unit
(LVA)

EDU

air spring rear

X-link valve rear axle

It is a good idea to understand how systems work before investigating them! This schematic drawing shows the air suspension on the L322. The 'X-link' or cross-link is the system that allows the independent suspension to behave like beam axles when off-road, to the benefit of traction.

Brakes

Disc brakes all round were standard on all varieties of L322. The Supercharged models always had Brembo brakes, which give excellent stopping power – they need to: this Range Rover is a heavy machine and is likely to get through a set of discs every 30,000 miles or so, or more frequently if it is driven hard. Pads may need more frequent replacement, so it is important to check when the brakes last had service attention. Don't just take the seller's word for it. Use your eyes and double-check in the sheaf of service documents that should accompany the vehicle.

Land Rovers traditionally had a handbrake that operated on the transmission, but buyers of luxury cars were often startled by the way these vehicles lurched very slightly when parked

The complex layout of the independent front suspension is visible here on a display model created for the launch in Britain in 2001. The front air springs are part of a strut assembly that incorporates the damper.

on a slope, as slack in the transmission was taken up. So the L322 Range Rover had a different system, there were parking brake drums integral with each rear disc, and the handbrake acted on these to eliminate that initial lurch. Beginning with the 2006 model-year, the handbrake was operated by an electric servo activated by a paddle switch on the centre console, and there was no conventional handbrake lever. This removed some clutter from the console area, but the electronic handbrake was prone to problems, including seizing in the 'on' position. Check that an electronic handbrake works correctly, and ask whether it has ever given trouble.

Remember that a new electronic handbrake module is expensive.

Steering ☑4 ☑3 ☑2 ☑1

The L322 was the first Range Rover to have rack-and-pinion steering. Earlier models did not because the directness of this type of system caused unpleasant feedback through the steering wheel during off-road driving on uneven surfaces. Careful design eliminated those problems for L322, and of course the steering was power-assisted as standard as well. When in tip-top condition, it is quite sharp and accurate (even though those transferring from sporty saloons tend to complain of vagueness).

The steering should feel quite direct, and it should not moan or hiss – although the mechanical parts of it may make protesting noises if the wheels are turned on a hard surface while the vehicle is stationary (as may happen in parking manoeuvres). If it falls short of the mark in any of these areas, suspect a problem.

Front disc brakes were ventilated from the start. The rear discs incorporate a drum for the handbrake.

To test for steering problems, you need an assistant to turn the steering wheel from lock to lock while you get under the vehicle and check for fluid leaks from the PAS box and for movement in the steering linkages. There is also, of course, a steering damper, which runs horizontally ahead of the front axle. If there are problems here, your road test will have revealed excessive vibration through the steering wheel.

Dampers ☑4 ☑3 ☑2 ☑1

It is difficult to test the dampers (shock absorbers) on a Range Rover by the sort of bounce test that people commonly used for cars. Worn dampers will, in any case, have been obvious during your test drive, so check now for fluid leaks or for damage to the casings. Note that the front dampers are integral with the suspension struts.

Propshafts ☑4 ☑3 ☑2 ☑1

Check for wear in the transmission by grasping the front and rear propshafts in turn and trying to twist them. They will turn slightly as slack in the system is taken up, but if either will rotate as much as a quarter of a turn, there is excessive wear. This may well be in the appropriate differential.

While looking at the transmission, check for wear in the universal joints in the propshaft by using a screwdriver as a lever to see if there is appreciable movement between the yoke and the joint. The more movement there is, the more advanced that wear will be.

Fuel tank, and LPG conversions ☑4 ☑3 ☑2 ☑1

All these Range Rovers have a plastic fuel tank mounted at the rear of the chassis that does not normally give trouble. However, it's wise to check the security of its fixings and for any signs of impact damage to the steel guard plates around it. This kind of damage can occur in heavy off-road use.

The cost of running a V8-engined Range Rover as an everyday vehicle has persuaded some owners to go for an LPG conversion. LPG has been subject to

Worth noting in this view of the rear suspension is the location of the universal joint in the propshaft forward of the differential.

lower taxation than petrol and, although it is slightly less energy-efficient, it can therefore considerably reduce fuel costs.

An LPG conversion will normally include an extra fuel tank, typically fitted into the spare wheel well (which means that the spare has to be carried somewhere else). A Range Rover converted to run on LPG normally retains the ability to run on petrol from the standard fuel tank as well. If an LPG system has been fitted, ask to see evidence that the system has been checked and approved as safe by an appropriate authority, if you didn't do so during your earlier inspection. Your insurers may well ask for an engineer's report, too.

Exhaust system 4️⃣ 3️⃣ 2️⃣ 1️⃣

All models of L322 Range Rover have a twin exhaust system, although obviously these vary from one engine type to another. The standard exhaust systems last for a long time, but suppliers of aftermarket systems sell a lot of 'sports' exhausts (typically tuned to make a more aggressive or interesting sound) and special exhaust tips (which are purely cosmetic).

The standard fuel tank is located behind the rear wheels, where it can be seen on this 'ghosted' drawing.

The vehicle you are evaluating may have one of these aftermarket systems, and whether you like it or not is entirely up to you. Very much worth having, of course, is an aftermarket stainless steel system, especially one to the original specifications. These last much better than mild steel systems, and you are unlikely ever to have to buy a new exhaust – which is a good thing, because they can be expensive. However, if the vendor tells you that such a system is fitted, it's wise to ask for evidence, such as an invoice, that the system really is stainless steel.

Whatever type of system is fitted, it's a good idea to check the mountings, both rigid and flexible. Few things are more annoying than an exhaust that bangs against the underside of the vehicle over bumps. And, of course, a broken mounting will put strain on the system and encourage its early demise.

While you're examining the exhaust, it's worth checking the state of the tailpipes, too. On diesel models, the inside of each exhaust pipe is always likely to be a black colour. On petrol models, a light grey deposit inside the pipe is a good sign, but a powdery black deposit suggests the engine is running rich, or that the vehicle has been used excessively in low-speed town traffic.

Interior

You checked for obvious signs of damage to the interior when you did your 15-minute assessment of the vehicle. The main task now is to check the electrical systems, and you may well need to do quite a lot of that, especially if your road test has revealed any potentially worrying messages or if there are warning lights that have not gone out as they should. Remember that the L322 is utterly dependent on its electronic systems, so you need to check the correct functioning of as many switches and buttons as you reasonably can.

Remember that these checks will be quite demanding of battery power, and that when the battery is drained and no longer puts out a full 12 volts, all kinds of systems start to misbehave and flash up warning lights or messages. Don't be surprised if the vendor gets a little bored while you're doing your checks, either; many owners have never explored all the systems on their own vehicles! As for the results, be realistic. You may be able to manage without certain convenience functions (although over time, their absence can become annoying). If you have an aptitude for chasing electrical problems yourself, you may be able to find them and fix them, but as soon as you entrust an L322 with electrical problems to a specialist, you can expect it to cost money.

It's simplest to divide your checks into two areas, one covering essentials and the other covering convenience features.

Essentials [4] [3] [2] [1]

Essentials are such things as the heating and ventilating systems (which you should have checked on the test drive), the electric windows, the power seat adjustment, the central locking, the mirror adjusters, and so on. Is there anything you would regularly use while driving that doesn't work? If so, deduct points.

The leather upholstery is normally robust, but check for excess wear on the driver's seat and, of course, for cuts and tears caused by carelessness. This is the semi-aniline leather in a 2009 Autobiography model. The wearing surfaces are perforated.

Convenience features [4] [3] [2] [1]

Convenience features are the things that it's nice to have working but, if not, won't prevent you from using the vehicle safely. All models of L322 Range Rover have a lot of them, because these high equipment levels enabled them to compete for sales in the luxury class with conventional saloons.

Life is really too short to go through every single option on the menu screen, and the vehicle's owner won't thank you if you try to do it. So just check a few functions, such as the satnav (you can always ask the vendor to explain how to set it, and watch what happens) and look out in general for faults in the screen displays, such as unwanted lines of 'interference' or elements that fail to display properly.

Checking the heating and ventilating controls is just the beginning of your examination of the vehicle's electrical systems. The centre stack on this 2009 model also has switches for the DSC traction control, the heated front seats, the heated front and rear screens, the radar parking sensors, and the tailgate release.

The centre screen has varied over the years as software and hardware have both been upgraded. This is the type used on the earliest models.

The whole monitor unit is physically different on this 2006 model, with different control buttons and switches. The screen is displaying the drivetrain information; it can be used to relay a graphic showing the behaviour of the suspension.

Has the satellite navigation system been updated recently? Updates cost about ⬤x150 but this is an expense that many owners think they can do without. If a rear seat entertainment system is fitted, with screens in the backs of the front-seat headrests, check that it works properly.

The engine bay

What you look for here will depend to a large extent on which engine is fitted. Don't forget that (assuming you took a test drive early on in this assessment), engine components will still be hot – and don't go whipping caps off radiator header tanks, for the same reason! As a matter of course, check the tension of the drive belts, and look for loose or frayed wiring. The cosmetic cover on every engine will hinder your access, but remember that it also helps to protect what's under it from damage. If the cosmetic cover is missing, you definitely need to find out why!

The engine bays of all L322 variants are very well filled, with the result that it is quite difficult to get a good look at the bulkhead, the inner wings and the wheel arches. However, it is always a good idea to have a gentle poke around in the less accessible areas to check for signs of debris building up – such as between the vertical and horizontal surfaces of the inner wings. Major build-ups of debris can absorb water and hold it against the metal

Yet another screen, again on a 2006 model: in this case, a rear seat entertainment system is fitted, and of course it is controlled from the dashboard monitor.

This is the rear entertainment system in a 2006 Autobiography model. Check that both the screens in the headrests actually work!

Electric windows are an absolute must to check carefully.

Seats have multi-way adjustment, and you need to make sure that all the servo motors do what they are designed to do.

There are even controls on the steering wheel to check ...

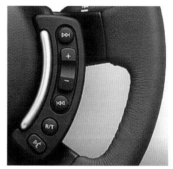

... on both sides!

The rotary gear selector on late models (this is on a 2011 model) is easy enough to check for correct operation.

The electronic parking brake must work correctly, and you should check the suspension height adjustment and that the transfer box servo motor has not seized. However, it's difficult to test whether all the functions of the Terrain Response system do what they were designed to do.

More buttons to press and investigate, this time on a Westminster edition from the 2009 model-year.

underneath, with some fairly predictable results in the longer term. Check where you can for any signs of rippled metal, which typically reveals that the vehicle has been in a collision (even though the repairs may be otherwise top-notch).

All variants have the battery concealed under a large plastic cover panel on the left of the engine bay as you stand looking into it. This cover does not come off easily, but is held in place by screws that you will have to remove (ask the owner's permission before you start, and explain what you are doing). Check for corrosion around the battery terminals (sometimes caused by them being less than fully tight), and check that the battery is of the correct rating: it should be either a 90 amp-hour or 110 amp-hour type on both petrol and diesel models. Original equipment batteries were sealed-for-life types.

Many owners fit larger-capacity batteries because battery drain can be a problem on Range Rovers that are left unused for several days at a time. Ask when the battery was last changed, and bear in mind that a weak battery can be the cause of multiple malfunctions and fault warnings on the dashboard message centre.

Now take a moment to check fluid levels. Oil is easily checked by the dipstick; coolant is easily checked by a look at the expansion tank; and the power steering reservoir has its own dipstick embedded in the screw cap. Double-check the coolant by looking for signs of leakage on and from the radiator, and bear in mind that the expansion tank can split – white streaks of coolant will reveal where this has occurred.

It is quite common to find that an engine – especially one of the diesels – has been tuned for greater power, typically by means of a replacement or 'piggy-back' ECU chip. Several aftermarket specialists have offered these, and a chip-tuned engine should not normally be a cause for concern, but bear in mind that owners have an engine chipped because they want extra performance, and that they are likely to have used that extra performance to the full.

Each engine has its own weaknesses, and it is worth knowing what they are. Note, though, that the sort of analysis you can carry out during an inspection of this sort will only give you a rough idea of the cause of a problem; in most cases, engine faults can only be identified precisely by hooking the vehicle up to proper electronic diagnostic equipment – and that is a job for a specialist workshop.

On all models, both petrol and diesel, beware of a rattle or a tinny sound from the exhaust when the engine is warm. This could indicate that the catalytic converter has broken up, and a replacement is expensive: from about ●x350 on a Td6 diesel to ●x930 on a TDV8 or a petrol V8. It may sound silly, but do check that the catalytic converters (two on some models) really are present, because there is a criminal trade in cutting them open and removing the precious metals inside. It should go without saying that the law requires them to be present on any vehicle that had them when new.

On all diesels, the DPF (Diesel Particulates Filter) can clog if the vehicle has only been driven for short distances. The DPF warning light will illuminate on the dashboard, the engine will lack power and may smoke, and there may be a strong smell of diesel. The problem can usually be cleared by a good long run in the vehicle.

Td6 diesel

These engines are usually reliable, but some suffered major failures early in their lives. Generally speaking, an engine that is healthy after 80,000 miles can be considered a good long-term proposition. On the test drive, misfires and roughness will indicate injector faults, and a whine will indicate that the turbocharger is on the way out. This is expensive to replace; budget for around ●x2500, including the labour from an independent specialist. A lack of power is likely to be caused by a faulty EGR (Exhaust Gas Recirculation) valve or by a split in one of the intercooler hoses.

BMW petrol V8

The biggest problem with these engines is leaks. The valve cover gaskets can give way, allowing quite major oil leaks down the side of the engine. Another common problem is failed O-ring seals at the water jacket housing at the back of the engine, which will lead to overheating. The coolant can also leak into the gearbox.

TDV8 diesel

The TDV8 diesel may develop turbocharger problems. Black smoke from the exhaust suggests that one of the intercooler hoses has split, and in such circumstances the electronics will typically put the engine into 'limp-home' (restricted performance) mode to protect it. If you suspect this problem, take a good look at the two hoses that run from the intercooler into the engine; squeezing a hose will open up a suspected split.

Supercharged engines

Listen carefully for a rattle from the supercharger while the engine is idling. Check also for exhaust system problems and double-check that there are no problems with the catalytic converters.

Paperwork and last-minute checks

You looked at the paperwork when you did your preliminary assessment. Now's the time to double-check that everything is in order, and do bear in mind that in order to understand the vehicle, you really do need the driver's handbook that was supplied with it when new. If it isn't present, use the fact to help haggle the price down a bit (these are thick volumes, and quite expensive from Land Rover), and then go and look for a handbook on the internet or at an auto jumble. Expect to pay ⬤x30 to ⬤x40 for a good secondhand one.

You should also make sure that there are two 'keys' – electronic fobs – with the vehicle. You only need one to drive it, but you need a spare in case you lose that, or to suit a second driver. These keys are expensive because they incorporate a transponder that is part of the anti-theft system; they can only be obtained through Land Rover dealerships, and they must be programmed ('synchronised') to suit the individual vehicle. Buying a secondhand key is simply not an option, because the keys cannot be re-programmed to suit a second vehicle.

Evaluation procedure

Add up the total points, and see what category the vehicle falls into. The maximum possible score is 100.

Score: 100 = excellent; 75 = good; 50 = average; 25 = poor.

Cars scoring over 70 will be completely usable and will require only maintenance and care to preserve condition. Cars scoring between 25 and 51 will require some serious work (at much the same cost regardless of score). Cars scoring between 52 and 69 will require very careful assessment of the necessary repair/restoration costs in order to arrive at a realistic value.

10 Auctions
– sold! Another way to buy your dream

Auction pros & cons
Pros: Prices will usually be lower than those of dealers or private sellers and you might grab a real bargain on the day. Auctioneers have usually established clear title with the seller. At the venue you can usually examine documentation relating to the vehicle.
Cons: You have to rely on a sketchy catalogue description of condition and history. The opportunity to inspect is limited and you cannot drive the car. Auction cars are often a little below par and may require some work. It's easy to overbid. There will usually be a 'buyer's premium' to pay in addition to the auction hammer price.

Which auction?
Auctions by established auctioneers are advertised in car magazines and on the auction houses' websites. A catalogue, or a simple printed list of the lots for auctions might only be available a day or two ahead, though lots are often listed and pictured on auctioneers' websites much earlier. Contact the auction company to ask if previous auction selling prices are available as this is useful information (details of past sales are often available on websites).

Catalogue, entry fee and payment details
When you purchase the catalogue of the vehicles in the auction, it often acts as a ticket allowing two people to attend the viewing days and the auction. Catalogue details tend to be comparatively brief, but will include information such as "one owner from new, low mileage, full service history," etc. It will also usually show a guide price to give you some idea of what to expect to pay and will tell you what is charged as a buyer's premium. The catalogue will also contain details of acceptable forms of payment. An immediate deposit is usually required at the fall of the hammer, the balance payable within 24 hours. If the plan is to pay by cash there may be a cash limit. Some auctions will accept payment by debit card, and sometimes credit or charge cards, but these will often incur an extra charge. A bank draft or bank transfer will have to be arranged in advance with your own bank as well as with the auction house. No vehicle will be released before all payments are cleared. If delays occur in payment transfers, then you can accrue storage costs.

Buyer's premium
A buyer's premium will be added to the hammer price: don't forget this in your calculations. It is also not usual for there to be a further state tax or local tax on the purchase price and/or on the buyer's premium.

Viewing
In some instances it's possible to view earlier in the day, or even days, before the auction, as well as in the hours prior to the car going under the hammer. There are auction officials available who are willing to help out by opening engine and luggage compartments, and to allow you to inspect the interior. While the officials may start the engine for you, a test drive is out of the question. Crawling under and around the car is permitted, but you can't suggest that the car you are interested in be jacked up, or attempt to do so yourself. You can also ask to see any documentation available.

Bidding

Before you take part in the auction, decide your maximum bid – and stick to it!

It may take a while for the auctioneer to reach the lot you are interested in, so use that time to observe how other bidders behave. When your car is up, attract the auctioneer's attention and make an early bid. The auctioneer will then look to you for a reaction every time another bid is made; usually the bids will be in fixed increments until the bidding slows, when smaller increments will often be accepted before the hammer falls. If you want to withdraw from the bidding, make sure the auctioneer understands your intentions – a vigorous shake of the head when he or she looks to you for the next bid should do the trick!

Assuming that you are the successful bidder, the auctioneer will note your card or paddle number, and from that moment on you will be responsible for the vehicle.

If the vehicle is unsold, either because it failed to reach the reserve or because there was little interest, it may be possible to negotiate with the owner, via the auctioneers, after the sale is over.

Successful bid

There are two more items to think about. How to get the Range Rover home, and insurance. If you can't drive the vehicle, a trailer is one way – either your own or hired; another is to have the vehicle shipped using the facilities of a local company. The auction house will also have details of companies specialising in the transfer of cars. Insurance for immediate cover can usually be purchased on site, but it may be more cost-effective to make arrangements with your own insurance company in advance, and then call to confirm the full details.

eBay & other online auctions?

eBay & other online auctions could land you a Range Rover L322 at a bargain price, though you'd be foolhardy to bid without examining it first, something most vendors encourage. A useful feature of eBay is that the geographical location of the vehicle is shown, so you can narrow your choices to those within a realistic radius of home. Be prepared to be outbid in the last few moments of the auction. Remember, your bid is binding and that it will be very, very difficult to get restitution in the case of a crooked vendor fleecing you – caveat emptor!

Be aware that some vehicles offered for sale in online auctions are 'ghost' cars. Don't part with any cash without being sure that the vehicle exists and is as described (usually pre-bidding inspection is possible).

Auctioneers

Barrett-Jackson	www.barrett-jackson.com/
Bonhams	www.bonhams.com/
British Car Auctions (BCA)	www.bca-europe.com/ or www.british-car-auctions.co.uk/
Cheffins	www.cheffins.co.uk/
Christie's	www.christies.com/
Coys	www.coys.co.uk/
eBay	www.eBay.com/
H&H	www.handh.co.uk/
RM	www.rmauctions.com/
Shannons	www.shannons.com.au/
Silver	www.silverauctions.com/

There is undeniably a certain excitement about the auction process, so keep your calm! This picture shows the first L322 ever to be auctioned – put through as a used vehicle by Land Rover to judge second-hand values very early in the model's life. (Courtesy *British Car Auctions*)

11 Paperwork
– correct documentation is essential!

The paper trail

Classic, collector, and prestige cars usually come with a large portfolio of paperwork accumulated and passed on by a succession of proud owners. This documentation represents the real history of the car, and from it you can deduce the level of care the car has received, how much it's been used, which specialists have worked on it, and the dates of major repairs and restorations. All of this information will be priceless to you as the new owner, so be very wary of cars with little paperwork to support their claimed history.

The Owner's Handbook is a very valuable document to have, and originally came in a smart branded wallet. This is an early example, with the supplementary handbooks for the service history and the audio, TV and navigation systems.

Registration documents

All countries/states have some form of registration for private vehicles whether its like the American 'pink slip' system or the British 'log book' system.

It is essential to check that the registration document is genuine, that it relates to the car in question, and that all the vehicle's details are correctly recorded, including chassis/VIN and engine numbers (if these are shown). If you are buying from the previous owner, their details will be recorded in the document; this will not be the case if you are buying from a dealer.

In the UK, the current (Euro-aligned) registration document is named 'V5C,' and is printed in coloured sections of blue, green, and pink. The blue section relates to the car specification, the green section has details of the new owner, and the pink section is sent to the DVLA in the UK when the car is sold. A small section in yellow deals with selling the car within the motor trade.

The DVLA will provide details of earlier keepers of the vehicle upon payment of a small fee, and much can be learned in this way.

If the car has a foreign registration there may be expensive and time-consuming formalities to complete. Do you really want the hassle?

Roadworthiness certificate

Most country/state administrations require that vehicles are regularly tested to prove that they are safe to use on the public highway and do not produce excessive emissions. In the UK that test (the 'MOT') is carried out at approved testing stations, for a fee. In the USA the requirement varies, but most states insist on an emissions test every two years as a minimum, and the police pulling over unsafe-looking vehicles.

In the UK the test is required on an annual basis after a vehicle is three years old. Of particular relevance for older cars is that the certificate issued includes the mileage reading recorded at the test date and, therefore, becomes an independent record of that car's history. Ask the seller if previous certificates are available. Without an MOT the vehicle should be trailered to its new home, unless you insist that a valid MOT is part of the deal (not a bad idea, as at least you will know the car was roadworthy on the day it was tested, plus you don't need to wait for the old certificate to expire before having the test done.)

Road licence

The administration of every country/state charges some kind of tax for the use of its road system: the actual form of the 'road licence,' and how it is displayed, varies enormously country to country and state to state.

Changed legislation in the UK means that the seller of a car must surrender any existing road fund licence, and it is the responsibility of the new owner to re-tax the vehicle at the time of purchase and before the car can be driven on the road. It's therefore vital to see the Vehicle Registration Certificate (V5C) at the time of purchase, and to have access to the New Keeper Supplement (V5C/2), allowing the buyer to obtain road tax immediately.

In the UK, if a car is untaxed because it has not been used for a period of time, the owner has to inform the licensing authorities, otherwise the vehicle's date-related registration number will be lost and there will be a painful amount of paperwork to get it re-registered.

Certificates of authenticity

For many makes of collectible car it is possible to get a certificate proving the age and authenticity (eg engine and chassis numbers, paint colour and trim) of a particular vehicle; these are sometimes called 'Heritage Certificates' and if the car comes with one of these it is a definite bonus. If you want to obtain one, the relevant owners' club is the best starting point.

Valuation certificate

In some cases, the vendor will have a recent valuation certificate or letter, signed by a recognised expert, stating how much he, or she, believes the particular car to be worth (such documents, together with photos, are usually needed to get 'agreed value' insurance). Generally, such documents should act only as confirmation of your own assessment of the car rather than a guarantee of value as the expert has probably not seen the car in the flesh. The easiest way to find out how to obtain a formal valuation is to contact the owners' club.

Service history

It is quite common for a Range Rover that has been owned by an enthusiast to have been serviced at home for several years – but bear in mind that the complex servicing requirements of an L322 Range Rover will usually have required some assistance from outside sooner or later. Nevertheless, try to obtain as much service history and other paperwork pertaining to the car as you can. Naturally, dealer stamps, or specialist garage receipts score most points in the value stakes. However, anything helps in the great authenticity game, items like the original bill of sale, handbook, parts invoices, and repair bills, adding to the story and the character of the car. Even a brochure correct to the year of the car's manufacture is a useful document, and something that you could well have to search hard to locate in future years. If the seller claims that the car has been restored, then expect receipts and other evidence from a specialist restorer.

This set of handbooks was supplied with a 2008 model, and is even more comprehensive than the earlier one. It's far better to get your information from these than to rely on asking other people through social media!

If the seller claims to have carried out regular servicing, ask what work was completed, when, and seek some evidence of it being carried out. Your assessment of the car's overall condition should tell you whether the seller's claims are genuine.

Restoration photographs
If the seller tells you that the vehicle has been restored, then expect to be shown a series of photographs taken while the restoration was under way. Pictures taken at various stages, and from various angles, should help you gauge the thoroughness of the work. If you buy the car, ask if you can have all the photographs as they form an important part of the vehicle's history. It's surprising how many sellers are happy to part with their car and accept your cash, but want to hang on to their photographs! In the latter event, you may be able to persuade the vendor to get a set of copies made.

12 What's it worth?

– let your head rule your heart

Condition

If the Range Rover you've been looking at is in poor condition, then you've probably not bothered to use the marking system in Chapter 9 – Serious evaluation. You may not even have got as far as using that chapter at all!

If you did use the marking system in Chapter 9 you'll know whether the Range Rover is in 'Excellent' (maybe Concours), 'Good,' 'Average,' or 'Poor' condition or, perhaps, somewhere in-between these categories.

Many specialist magazines run a regular price guide. If you haven't bought the latest editions, do so now and compare their suggested values for the model you are thinking of buying; also look at the auction prices if they are reporting these.

At the time of writing, L322 Range Rover values generally remained quite strong because the later models still retained plenty of prestige value and many were still in use as ordinary, everyday transport. Values for earlier examples had started to tumble, though, which was making the model more attractive to enthusiasts.

The values published in the magazines tend to vary from one magazine to another, as do their scales of condition, so read the guidance notes they provide carefully. Bear in mind that a really top-class, low-mileage L322 Range Rover could be worth more than the highest scale published. Assuming that the one you have in mind is not one of these, then relate the level of condition that you judge it to be in with the appropriate guide price. How does the figure compare with the asking price?

Before you start haggling with the seller, consider what effect any variation from standard specification might have on the car's value. If you are buying from a dealer, remember there will be a dealer's premium on the price.

This style of front wing vent was used on the later supercharged models, and some owners have added them to non-supercharged cars as well. Do modifications like this appeal to you, or not? Don't be persuaded to pay extra because of them.

Desirable options/extras

Many owners consider the most desirable vehicles to be the better-equipped ones, but the fact is that all L322 Range Rovers are highly-equipped: it was Land Rover's policy to offer a very wide choice of options (the idea was promoted as the 'Made for Me' concept) so that when the model reached showrooms in 2002 there were 1.8 million possible different combinations. Many of these were probably never actually built, but the figure gives some idea of why no two L322s you look at may have the same specification.

Once the vehicles entered the used car market, many owners fitted such things as the side vents from the Supercharged models, or newer (and, typically, larger) wheels, to make their vehicles look more prestigious and individualised. So the specification that one of these models has now may well not be the one with which it left the factory.

You might come across an ex-Police Range Rover; several UK forces used them as motorway cars. Generally speaking, they will have been well looked after, but will also have a high mileage and bear the scars of additional equipment, such as lights and radios. But the price may be temptingly low ...

Undesirable features

What is desirable and what is undesirable in an L322 Range Rover is governed by what you intend to do with the vehicle. At the time of writing, though, these vehicles are not generally being bought for hard recreational off-road use. (They are certainly capable of it, but the cost of repairing accidental damage remains a major deterrent; they are also too big for certain types of recreational off-road use.) You are, therefore, unlikely to find one that has been modified purely for that purpose.

Generally speaking, all non-original features will detract from a vehicle's value – and some buyers will be very wary of vehicles fitted with aftermarket accessories rather than genuine Land Rover items. Whether you want aftermarket accessories that are contemporary with the vehicle is a matter of personal choice. Arguably, they were part of the way it was when new or nearly new. Another argument is that they were not fitted by the factory or one of its dealers and are therefore not 'original' – and for an enthusiast that may be a deciding factor.

Striking a deal

Negotiate on the basis of your condition assessment, mileage, and fault rectification cost. Also take into account the Range Rover's specification. Be realistic about the value, but don't be completely intractable: a small compromise on the part of the vendor or buyer will often facilitate a deal at little real cost.

Limited Editions have their own appeal, but it is up to you to decide whether they have enough of that appeal to be worth more than a more 'standard' model.

Tempting, isn't it? This is the beautifully finished passenger cabin of a 35th Anniversary model. Is it worth more to you than the broadly similar interior of an HSE?

Land Rover offered a wide range of accessories when the L322 was new, including such items as this headlamp guard. If a vehicle has such things fitted, that's fine – but don't be talked into paying extra for them.

13 Do you really want to restore?
– it'll take longer and cost more than you think

Generally speaking, at the time of writing, L322 Range Rovers were not being bought by enthusiasts for restoration. They were more likely to be bought by those who admired their specification and abilities when they were new, and who wanted to enjoy some of the prestige that accompanies a Range Rover. Nevertheless, there is no doubt that there will be restorations in the years to come – although, as is always the case with luxury cars that were expensive when new, the costs of such restorations are going to be high.

However, you may have found an L322 that you find particularly interesting and that you believe deserves to be restored to the way it was when new. Perhaps it was owned by a relative and has some special meaning to you; perhaps it's a rare special edition and you appreciate its differences from the run-of-the-mill models; perhaps you just like it, and want to restore it to its former glory – an expression which has become a cliché among car enthusiasts and usually implies spending a lot of money!

Be realistic about what you are able achieve. Easiest of all is a rolling restoration, which means that the vehicle remains usable for most of the time, and that you improve it in larger or smaller bites as you go along. Hardest of all is the complete restoration of a derelict vehicle – at the time of writing, this was extremely uncommon, if only because very few vehicles had reached that state.

Cost will play a very big part in what you do. It has long been a maxim in the classic vehicle world that any restoration will take twice as long and cost at least twice as much as your original, hard-headed estimate. And forget the idea that you will be able to sell the completed vehicle for more than you have spent on it. Prices could rise that much in the next few years, but it's much more likely that they won't.

So, if you decide to restore an L322 Range Rover, restore it for yourself. Restore it to your standards, to your time-scale, and to your budget. Even if you have the skills, the equipment and the premises to do the job, resign yourself to having no free weekends for at least a couple of years. If you don't have all these vital elements and are paying somebody else to do the work, resign yourself to having no money to spend on anything else for a similar period of time: Land Rover specialists and restorers can and do charge handsomely for deploying their skills. And whichever way you decide to go, resign yourself to frustrating waits while vital parts are sourced – or, in a worst case, re-made from scratch.

But don't let all this put you off. It's just a look on the bleak side to provoke you into thinking hard about what you're getting into. If you really are committed to getting that Range Rover up and running and looking the way you think it should, then the time, effort, and money will all be worth it in the end. And after that, every little improvement you make will make you feel prouder and prouder. It may well become a long-term commitment, but you'll almost certainly find that it's worth it. To you, at least.

If you aim to restore your Range Rover to the way it was when new, a good place to start is a sales brochure from the time. Make sure you get the right one for the model-year of your vehicle! Such items turn up at autojumbles and on eBay from time to time – but be careful, because some sellers think anything related to Range Rover is automatically worth a lot of money.

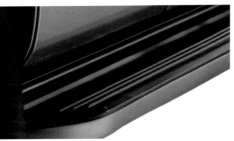

Some owners like to add extras during a restoration or refurbishment. A favourite of owners – and no doubt eventually of restorers too – is these bright-finish side vents. You may have trouble finding them in years to come, though.

Side steps are a valuable addition if regular occupants of your Range Rover find it too high off the ground for easy access. Land Rover offered a set as an accessory.

Also a Land Rover accessory, although much more expensive and much rarer, were these retractable side steps. They come with an ECU (different between pre- and post-2010 models) and have to be plumbed into the vehicle's electrical system.

These side protection bars were a genuine Land Rover accessory, but one that was never very popular in Britain. Also shown here are the lower-body bump rubbers; again, few people felt they were necessary.

14 Paint problems
– bad complexion, including dimples, pimples and bubbles

Paint faults generally occur due to lack of protection/maintenance, or poor preparation prior to a respray or touch-up. Some of the following conditions may be present in the car you're looking at:

Orange peel
This appears as an uneven paint surface, similar to the appearance of the skin of an orange. The fault is caused by the failure of atomized paint droplets to flow into each other when they hit the surface. It's sometimes possible to rub out the effect with proprietary paint cutting/ rubbing compound or very fine grades of abrasive paper. A respray may be necessary in severe cases. Consult a bodywork repairer/paint shop for advice on the particular car.

Cracking
Severe cases are likely to have been caused by too heavy an application of paint (or filler beneath the paint). Also, insufficient stirring of the paint before application can lead to the components being improperly mixed, and cracking can result. Incompatibility with the paint already on the panel can have a similar effect. To rectify the problem it is necessary to rub down to a smooth, sound finish before respraying the problem area.

Crazing
Sometimes the paint takes on a crazed rather than a cracked appearance when the problems mentioned under 'Cracking' are present. This problem can also be caused by a reaction between the underlying surface and the paint. Paint removal and respraying the problem area is usually the only solution.

Blistering
Almost always caused by corrosion of the metal beneath the paint.
Usually perforation will be found in the metal and the damage will usually be worse than that suggested by the area of blistering. The metal will have to be repaired before repainting.

Micro blistering

Usually the result of an economy respray where inadequate heating has allowed moisture to settle on the car before spraying. Consult a paint specialist, but usually damaged paint will have to be removed before partial or full respraying. Can also be caused by car covers that don't 'breathe'.

Fading

Some colours, especially reds, are prone to fading if subjected to strong sunlight for long periods without the benefit of polish protection.

Sometimes proprietary paint restorers and/or paint cutting/rubbing compounds will retrieve the situation. Often a respray is the only real solution.

Peeling

Often a problem with metallic paintwork when the sealing lacquer becomes damaged and begins to peel off. Poorly applied paint may also peel. The remedy is to strip and start again!

Dimples

Dimples in the paintwork are caused by the residue of polish (particularly silicone types) not being removed properly before respraying. Paint removal and repainting is the only solution.

Dents

Small dents are usually easily cured by the 'Dentmaster,' or equivalent process, that sucks or pushes out the dent (as long as the paint surface is still intact). Companies offering dent removal services will usually come to your home: consult your telephone directory.

15 Problems due to lack of use
– just like their owners, Range Rovers need exercise!

A run of at least ten miles, once a week, is recommended for a L322 Range Rover.

Seized components
Pistons in callipers, and slave and master cylinders can seize; as will the clutch if the plate becomes stuck to the flywheel because of corrosion. Handbrakes (parking brakes) can seize if the cables and linkages rust. Pistons can seize in the bores due to corrosion.

Fluids
Old, acidic oil can corrode bearings; uninhibited coolant can corrode internal waterways; lack of antifreeze can cause cracks in the block or head, and push core plugs out; and silt settling and solidifying can cause overheating.

Brake fluid absorbs water from the atmosphere and should be renewed every two years. Old fluid with a high water content can seize (freeze) pistons/callipers due to corrosion, and brake failure when the water turns to vapour near hot components.

Tyre problems
Tyres unused for too long develop flat spots from the car's weight, causing some (usually temporary) vibration. If tyre walls have cracks or (blister-type) bulges, new tyres are needed.

Shock absorbers (dampers)
With lack of use, the dampers will lose their elasticity, or even seize. Creaking, groaning, and stiff suspension are signs of this problem.

Rubber and plastic
Radiator hoses can perish and split, possibly resulting in the loss of coolant. Window and door seals can harden and leak, gaiters/boots can crack, and wiper blades will harden.

Electrics
Some of the electrical equipment on an L322 depends on a constant 12-volt supply; a variety of faults will be recorded in the vehicle's 'brain' if the voltage drops too low. Any Range Rover that has been unused for a long time is likely to suffer problems, and will almost certainly require the attention of a specialist before it can be expected to function properly again. At the very least, it'll need a new battery, as the old one will probably be of little use if it has not been charged for many months.

Earthing/grounding problems are common when connections corrode. In an unused petrol engine, sparkplug electrodes often corrode. Wiring insulation can harden and fail.

Rotting exhaust system
Exhaust gas contains a high water content, so exhaust systems corrode very quickly from the inside when the vehicle is not used.

Air suspension
All L322 Range Rovers have air suspension, and you should expect to replace the air springs on a vehicle that has been unused for some time. Height sensors, compressor, and air reservoir may all need to be replaced as well before the system will work properly.

16 The Community

– key people, organisations and companies in the Range Rover world

The L322 Range Rover attracts a wide variety of devotees. There are those who like it for its prestige value (which will inevitably diminish with time: it was replaced by a new model in 2012). There are those who admire it for its breadth of abilities, which include off-road capability far beyond that of any other luxury car. And there is a growing number of enthusiasts who like it as a classic vehicle of its kind, in exactly the same way as there are enthusiasts for other classic cars.

However, it is always important to remember that this is a complex vehicle that does not take very kindly to DIY maintenance. It needs specialist attention, and even some independent Land Rover workshops prefer not to work on an L322 simply because of its complexity. Some of the more commonly needed spares are now becoming available through specialist parts suppliers, but in many cases it is still necessary to go to a Land Rover franchised dealership to obtain what is necessary.

The lists here are confined to the UK for space reasons, but even then they are very far from exhaustive. For details of clubs, specialists and suppliers in other countries, please consult your favourite 4x4 or Land Rover magazine, or check on the internet.

Clubs and the internet

It's worth knowing that there are multiple L322-focussed websites, internet forums, and Facebook pages out there waiting to be found. Whatever problem you have with an L322, it is almost certain that somebody else will have had it before, and has put the benefit of his or her experience online to aid fellow sufferers. But use these resources with care: some of them attract the opinionated rather than the knowledgeable, and you need to be able to distinguish between the two.

As a support network, the internet has largely taken over the role of the traditional enthusiasts' club. There is nevertheless nothing quite like meeting fellow owners face-to-face to share problems and advice, and there is one traditional club that is dedicated to Range Rovers of all types (and not just the L322 models).

This is the Range Rover Register, which can be found online at www.rrr.co.uk and contacted by telephone on 01908 667901.

Very much a part of the enthusiast scene is the G4 Owners' Club, which caters for all Land Rover vehicles that featured in the G4 Challenge adventure competition events, and that, of course, includes those L322 Range Rovers specially prepared for the job. You can find this club at www.g4ownersclub.com

There are also many local and regional Land Rover clubs in the UK, but at the time of writing not many of them have members who own L322 Range Rovers.

Hopefully the L322's time will come, but the Land Rover community has traditionally depended heavily on DIY fettling, which is much less possible

The L322 is a formidably competent off-road vehicle, but its size and cost have not endeared it to traditional off-roading enthusiasts.

Like all Land Rovers, the L322 Range Rover was built to cope with desert conditions, but adventurers and explorers tend to prefer vehicles that are simpler to repair if they break down.

Several examples of the L322 were used on the G4 Challenge adventure competition in 2003, and then as support vehicles on the 2006 event. This one has a front protection bar and special roof rack, plus additional equipment.

with an L322 than on most earlier models. Note, too, that the emphasis of many local clubs is on off-road driving (typically 'green laning') or on competitive motor sport (typically trialling) rather than on meticulous restoration for what US enthusiasts call 'show'n'shine' events. Some clubs of course cater for all forms of the hobby.

Main spares suppliers

At the time of writing, most spares for L322 models were supplied through Land Rover's own outlets. However, an increasing number of independent suppliers had also begun to cater for these models, and this list shows only the major ones.

John Craddock Ltd
North Street, Bridgtown, Cannock, Staffordshire, WS11 0AZ
01543 577207
www.johncraddockltd.co.uk

British Parts UK
Wedgewood Way, Stevenage, Hertfordshire , SG1 4QR
01438 354810
www.britishparts.co.uk

Brookwells Supplies,
Pottery Road, Bovey Tracey, Devon, TQ13 9DS
     or
3 Chantry Court, Marshall Road, Cothill, Plympton, Devon, PL7 1YB
01636 832555
www.brookwell.co.uk

LR Centre Ltd
Bridge Estate, Speke Hall Road, Speke, Liverpool, L24 9HB
0151 486 0066
www.lrparts.net

Paddock Spares and Accessories
The Showground, The Cliff, Matlock, Derbyshire, DE4 5EW
01629 760877
www.paddockspares.com

Rimmer Brothers

Triumph House, Sleaford Road, Bracebridge Heath, Lincoln, LN4 2NA
01522 568000
www.rimmerbros.co.uk

Specialist restorers

At the time of writing, few owners were prepared to spend large sums of money on restoration or refurbishment of an L322 Range Rover. As a result, there is a lack of specialist restorers in the trade. However, as demand increases, it is inevitable that specialist workshops will begin to cater for it.

In the mean time, any competent independent Land Rover workshop will probably be prepared to discuss major refurbishment of an L322 Range Rover – although many of the smaller ones will be rather wary of the task.

Vehicle information

Land Rover kept a detailed build record for every L322 Range Rover, and also keeps a central record of service work carried out on each example by its own dealers. This information is available through the Customer Relations Division, which can be contacted on 02476 56460. You will, of course, need to prove that you have a legitimate reason for wanting the information.

In Europe, details of earlier owners are protected by the General Data Protection Regulation, and you may be unable to find this information easily.

Magazines

Land Rover Monthly
The Publishing House
2 Brickfields Business Park
Woolpit
Suffolk
IP30 9QS
www.lrm.co.uk

Land Rover Owner International
Bauer
Media House
Lynchwood
Peterborough
PE2 6EA
www.lro.com

Books

Range Rover, 40 Years of the 4x4 Icon
by James Taylor
The Crowood Press Ltd
ISBN 978-1-84797-184-5

Range Rover. The Anniversary Guide
by Mike Gould
Porter Press International
ISBN 978-1-907085-05-5

In action! This picture was taken on the 2003 G4 Challenge event. Note the self-recovery winch mounted to the front bumper.

17 Vital statistics

– essential data at your fingertips

Production history

It helps to understand what you're looking at if you have some idea of how the Range Rover L322 evolved during its ten years in production. So here's a breakdown of the key changes; there were many more minor ones.

2002	February	Introduced, with 174bhp 3.0-litre BMW turbocharged Td6 diesel or 282bhp BMW 4.4-litre V8 petrol engines; five-speed automatic gearbox standard.
2005	May	New 306bhp 4.4-litre Jaguar V8 petrol and 390bhp 4.2-litre Jaguar supercharged V8 petrol engines introduced, both with six-speed automatic gearbox; BMW 3.0-litre diesel remains available with five-speed automatic gearbox; facelift with headlights 'cut into' grille for all models.
2006	November	New 268bhp 3.6-litre TDV8 diesel replaced 3.0-litre Td6.
2007	Autumn	Naturally-aspirated V8 petrol engine withdrawn from sale in Europe, but still available in USA and the Middle East.
2009	June	New 375bhp 5.0-litre Jaguar V8 petrol and 510bhp 5.0-litre supercharged V8 petrol replaced 4.4-litre and 4.2-litre engines respectively; second facelift, including three-element grille and daytime running lamps.
2010	June	New 308bhp 4.4-litre TDV8 diesel replaced 3.6-litre size; eight-speed automatic gearbox for new TDV8, but others retained the six-speed type.
2012	July	Last L322 Range Rover built.
2012	September	L405 replacement model announced.

Chassis numbers

All second-generation Range Rover models had VIN-type chassis numbers consisting of 17 digits. The last six digits were the serial number and the first 11 contain information about the specification. Note that there were differences between the 'RoW' (Rest of the World) codes and the 'NAS' (North American Specification) codes.
     The RoW codes break down like this:

SAL	Manufacturer code (Rover Group)
LM	Range Rover L322
A	Standard (113.4-inch) wheelbase
M	Four-door body

Engine: A = 4.4-litre BMW V8 petrol engine
C = 3.0-litre Td6 diesel engine
D = 5.0-litre LR-V8 petrol engine
E = 5.0-litre LR-V8 supercharged petrol engine
2 = 3.6-litre TDV8 diesel engine
3 = 4.2-litre supercharged V8 engine
5 = 4.4-litre Jaguar V8 petrol engine
7 = 3.6-litre TDV8 diesel engine with DPF

Drive: 3 = RHD with automatic gearbox
2 = LHD, automatic

Model year: 2 = 2002

3 = 2003	8 = 2008
4 = 2004	9 = 2009
5 = 2005	A = 2010
6 = 2006	B = 2011
7 = 2007	C = 2012

A = Assembled at Solihull

The VIN of an L322 Range Rover will be found on this tamper-proof sticker attached to the front inner wing, just ahead of the bulkhead. You may have to move some of the wiring out of the way to read it fully!

The NAS (North American Specification) prefix codes differed, as follows:

SAL = Manufacturer code (Land Rover)
M = Range Rover L322

Class: A = Class E, standard
B = Class E, HSE specification
E = Class E, HSE specification with special features (model-year dependent)
F = Class E, HSE specification with special features (model-year dependent)
H = Westminster Edition
1 = Four-door body

Engine: A = 4.4-litre BMW V8 petrol engine
D = 5.0-litre LR-V8 petrol engine
E = 5.0-litre LR-V8 supercharged petrol engine
3 = 4.2-litre supercharged V8 engine
5 = 4.4-litre Jaguar V8 petrol engine
2 = LHD with automatic gearbox
1 = Security check digit (0 to 9, or X)

Model year: 2 = 2002

3 = 2003	8 = 2008
4 = 2004	9 = 2009
5 = 2005	A = 2010
6 = 2006	B = 2011
7 = 2007	C = 2012

A = Assembled at Solihull

The VIN will also be found on a small panel visible through the base of the windscreen. Needless to say, the two numbers should be the same, and should tie up with the information on the vehicle's identity document! This one is SALLMAMC36A225241, which decodes as a 2006-model Td6 diesel with right-hand drive.

The Essential Buyer's Guide™ series ...

Also from Veloce Publishing ...

ISBN: 978-1-845850-14-2
Paperback • 19.5x13.9cm • 64 pages
• 106 pictures

ISBN: 978-1-787113-39-8
Paperback • 19.5x13.9cm • 64 pages
• 113 pictures

ISBN: 978-1-787112-22-3
Paperback • 19.5x13.9cm • 64 pages
• 105 pictures

ISBN: 978-1-787114-32-6
Paperback • 19.5x13.9cm • 64 pages
• 100 pictures

For more information and price details, visit our website at www.veloce.co.uk
email: info@veloce.co.uk • Tel: +44(0)1305 260068

More from James Taylor ...

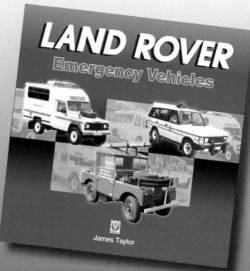

ISBN: 978-1-787112-44-5
Hardback • 25x25cm
• 144 pages • 367 pictures

ISBN: 978-1-787112-40-7
Hardback • 25x25cm
• 176 pages • 267 pictures

For more information and price details, visit our website at www.veloce.co.uk
email: info@veloce.co.uk • Tel: +44(0)1305 260068

Index